© Copyright 2021 - All rights reserved.

You may not reproduce, duplicate or send the contents of this book without direct written permission from the author. You cannot hereby despite any circumstance blame the publisher or hold him or her to legal responsibility for any reparation, compensations, or monetary forfeiture owing to the information included herein, either in a direct or an indirect way.

Legal Notice: This book has copyright protection. You can use the book for personal purpose. You should not sell, use, alter, distribute, quote, take excerpts or paraphrase in part or whole the material contained in this book without obtaining the permission of the author first.

Disclaimer Notice: You must take note that the information in this document is for casual reading and entertainment purposes only. We have made every attempt to provide accurate, up to date and reliable information. We do not express or imply guarantees of any kind. The persons who read admit that the writer is not occupied in giving legal, financial, medical or other advice. We put this book content by sourcing various places.

Please consult a licensed professional before you try any techniques shown in this book. By going through this document, the book lover comes to an agreement that under no situation is the author accountable for any forfeiture, direct or indirect, which they may incur because of the use of material contained in this document, including, but not limited to, — errors, omissions, or inaccuracies.

MANDALA

BIRDS COLORING BOOK
FOR ADULTS RELAXATION

"Don't seek, don't search, don't ask, don't knock, don't demand – relax."
Osho

"Don't be afraid to give up the good to go for the great."
John D. Rockefeller

"The purpose of our lives is to be happy"
Dalai Lama

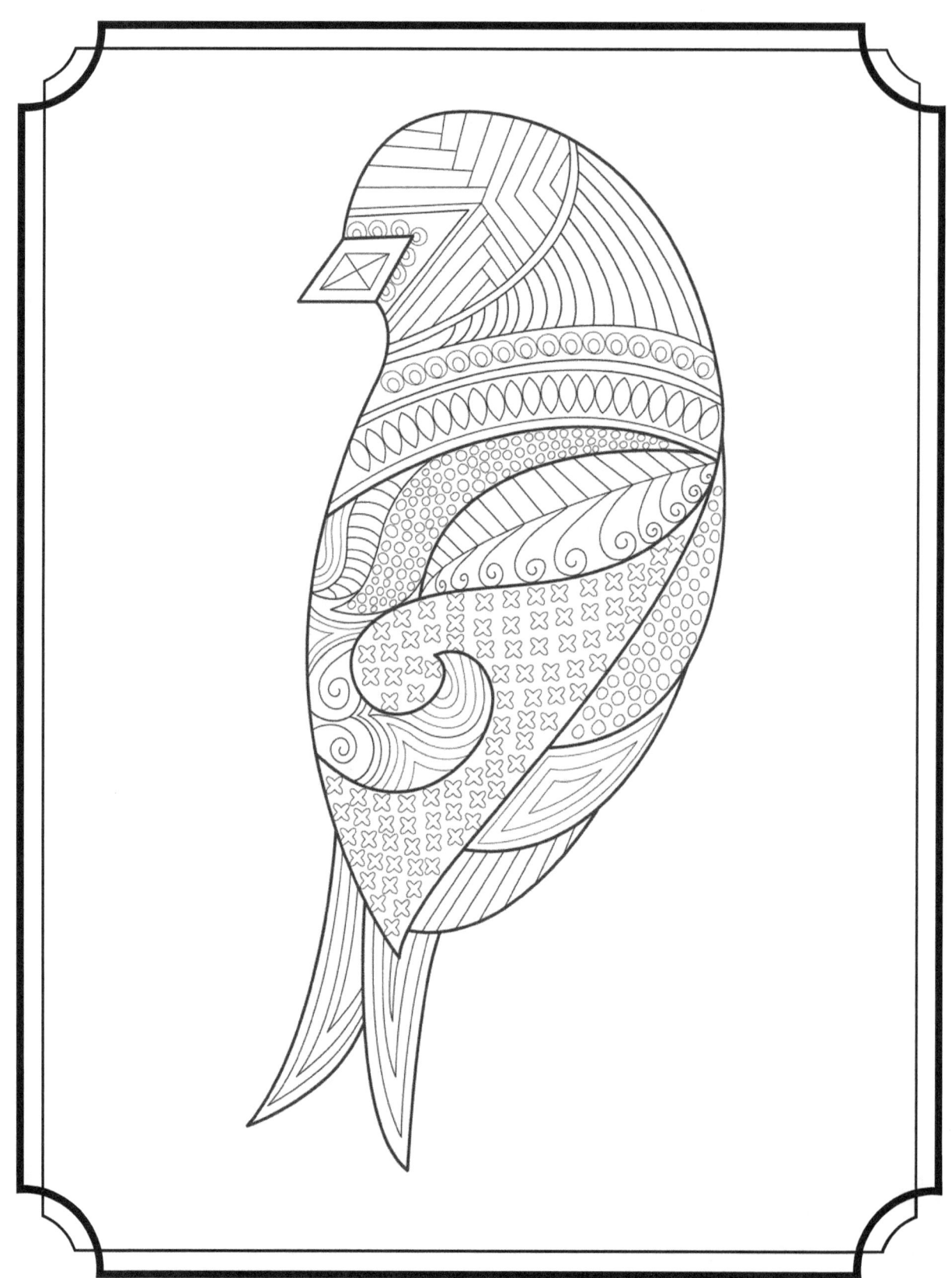

"The secret of getting ahead is getting started."
Mark Twain

"All our dreams can come true, if we have the courage to pursue them."
Walt Disney

The obstacle is the path.

-Zen saying

"Know that people are doing the best they can from their level of awareness. Accept people for who they are and always be ready to forgive."
Deepak Chopra

"Yesterday I was clever and wanted to change the world. Today I am wise so I am changing myself."
Rumi

"Only when you can be extremely pliable and soft can you be extremely hard and strong."
Zen Proverb

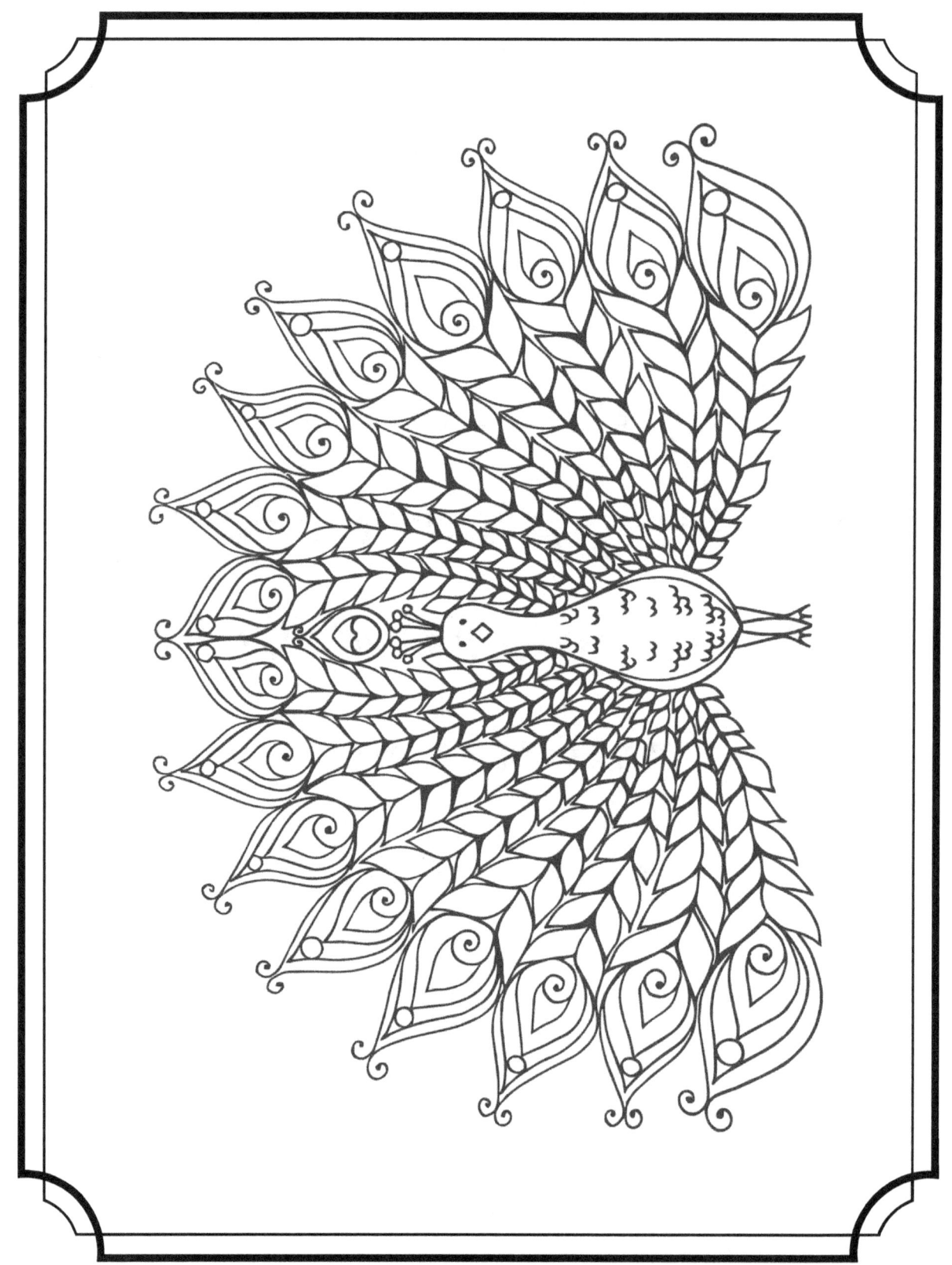

"When you realize nothing is lacking, the whole world belongs to you."
Lao Tzu

"Zen is not some kind of excitement, but concentration on our usual everyday routine."
Shunryu Suzuki

"Each morning, we are born again. What we do today is what matters most."

Buddha

"Who you are is always right."
Ming Dao Deng

Peace of mind is that mental condition in which you have accepted the worst.
Lin Yutang

"I don't mind what happens. That is the essence of inner freedom."

Jiddu Krishnamurti

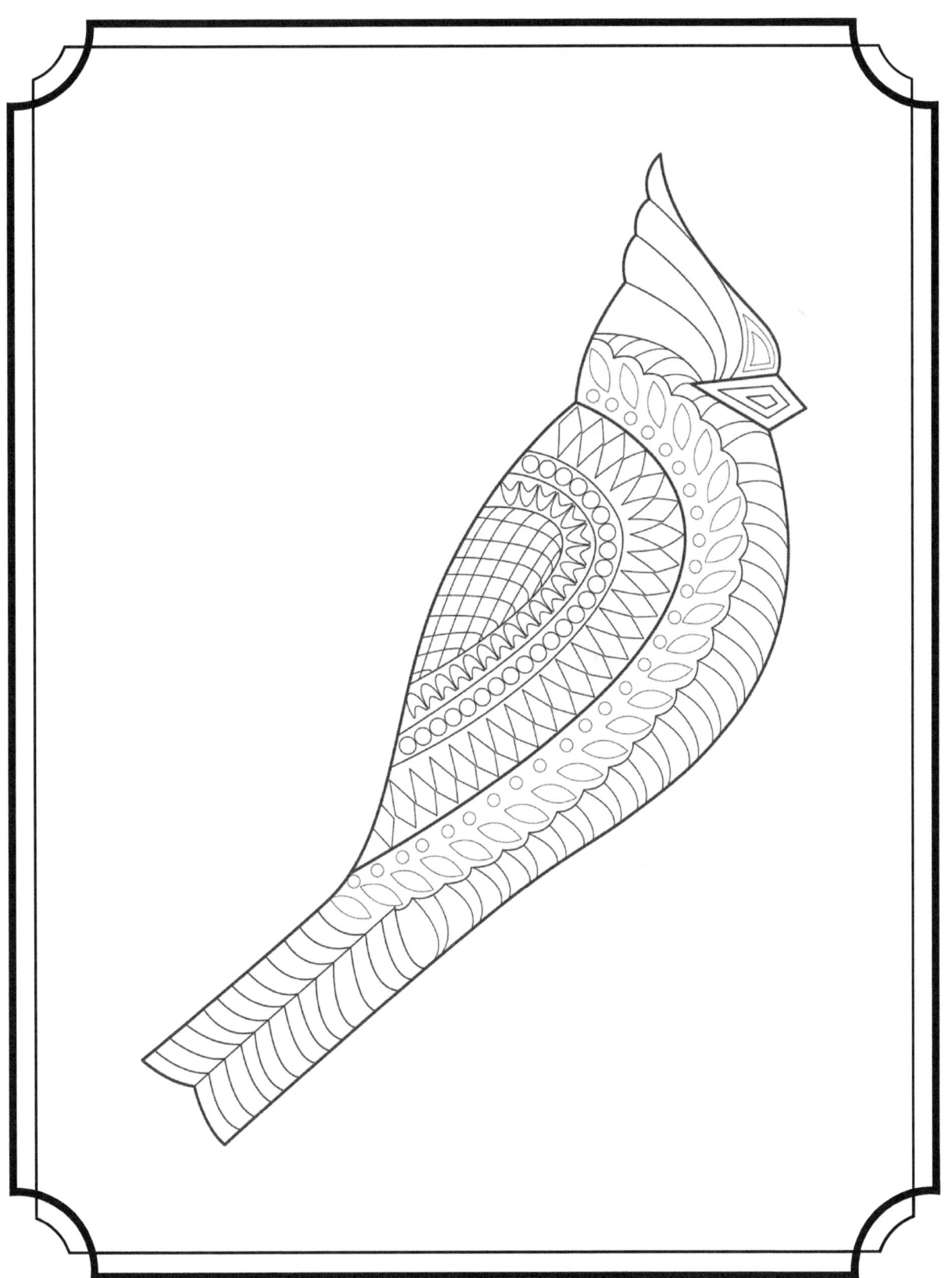

"Have the fearless attitude of a hero and the loving heart of a child."

Soyen Shaku

"Fear is a natural reaction to moving closer to the truth."
Prema Chödrön

"Do not follow the idea of others, but learn to listen to the voice within yourself."
Dōgen Zenji

"Do not dwell in the past, do not dream of the future, concentrate the mind on the present moment."
Buddha

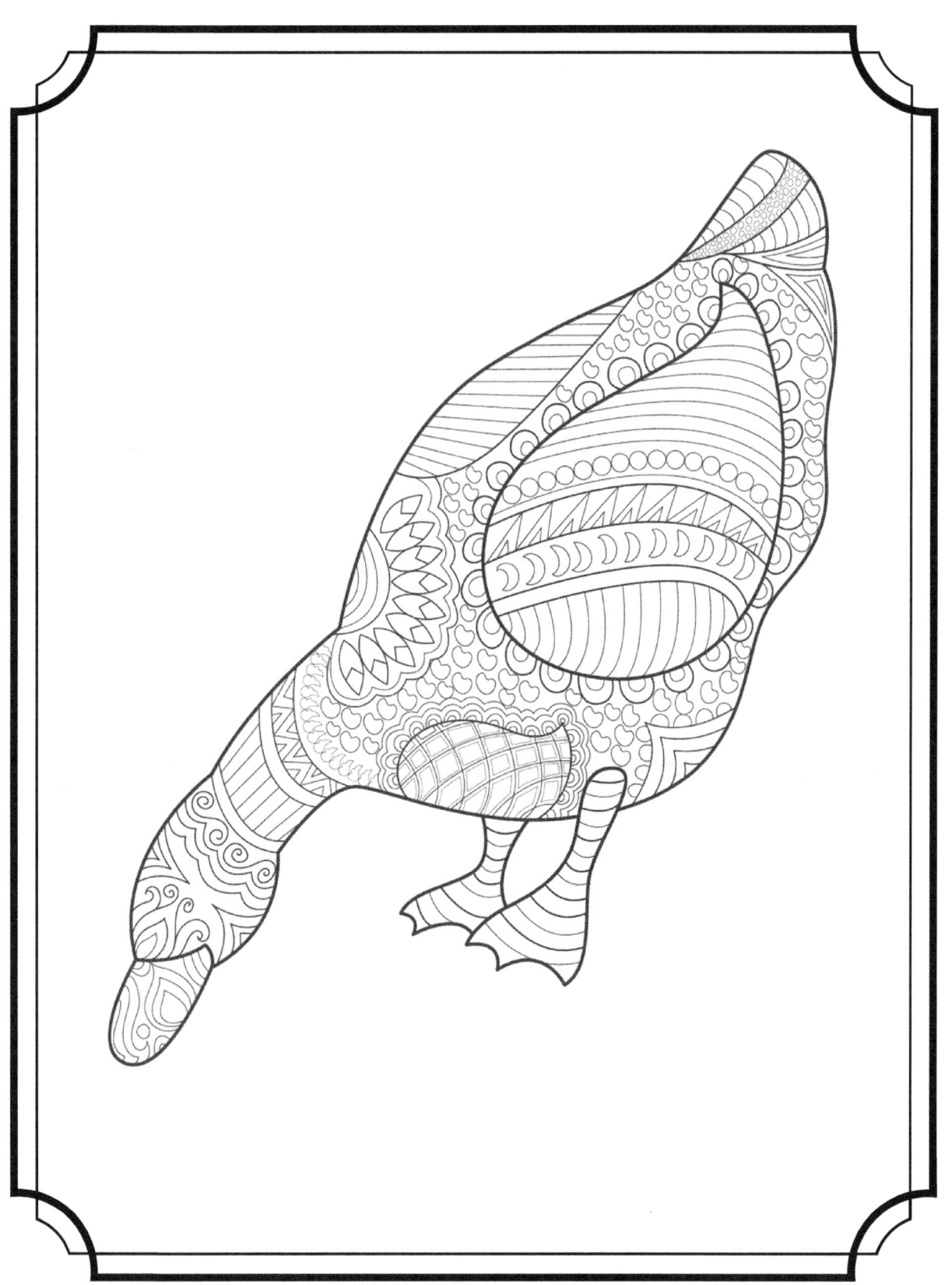

"If you are depressed, you are living in the past. If you are anxious, you are living in the future. If you are at peace, you are living in the present."
Lao Tzu

"Nothing ever exists entirely alone. Everything is in relation to everything else."
Buddha

"Wisdom says we are nothing. Love says we are everything. Between these two our life flows."
Jack Kornfield

"Wise men don't judge -
they seek to understand."
Wei Wu Wei

"The real meditation is how you live your life."
Jon Kabat-Zinn

"To be beautiful means to be yourself. You don't need to be accepted by others. You need to accept yourself."
Thích Nhất Hạnh

"Act without expectation."
Lao Tzu

"If you realize you have enough, you are truly rich."
Lao Tzu

"All that we are, is the result of what we have thought. The mind is everything. What we think, we become."
Buddha

"Have good trust in yourself ... not in the One that you think you should be, but in the One that you are."
Maezumi Roshi

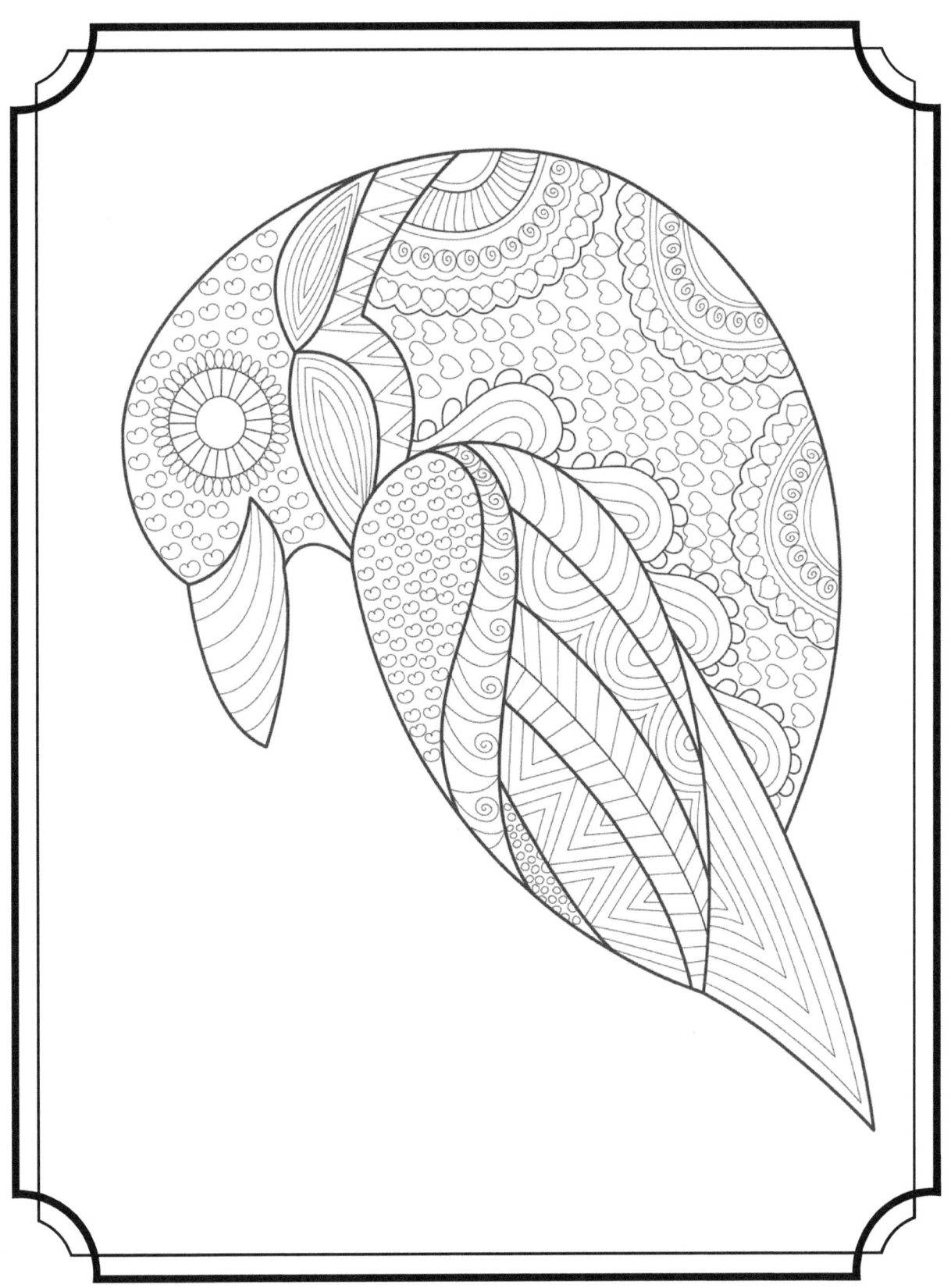

"Every experience is a lesson. Every loss is a gain."
Sathya Sai Baba

"Awareness is the greatest agent for change."

Eckhart Tolle

"Act without expectation."
Lao Tzu

"To be beautiful means to be yourself. You don't need to be accepted by others. You need to accept yourself."
Thich Nhất Hạnh

"The real meditation is how you live your life."
Jon Kabat-Zinn

"I don't mind what happens. That is the essence of inner freedom."

Jiddu Krishnamurti

Peace of mind is that mental condition in which you have accepted the worst.

Lin Yutang

Thank you !
We hope you enjoyed this book and had a lot of quality time. Your opinion is very important to us. Please let us know how you like this book at:

esilvia76@yahoo.com

www.ingramcontent.com/pod-product-compliance
Lightning Source LLC
Chambersburg PA
CBHW081349070526
44578CB00005B/778